The Social Tigress

Dating Advice for Women to Attract Men and Get a Boyfriend

D1304515

By Gregg Michaelsen

The Social Tigress
Dating Advice for Women to Attract Men and Get a Boyfriend!

By Gregg Michaelsen
"Confidence Builder"

DISCLAIMER: As a male dating coach I am very good at what I do because of my years of studying the nuances of interpersonal relationships. I have helped thousands of women understand men.

That said, I am not a psychologist, doctor or licensed professional. So do not use my advice as a substitute if you need professional help.

Women tell me how much I have helped them and I truly hope that I can HELP you too in your pursuit of that extraordinary man! I will provide you with powerful tools. YOU need to bring me your willingness to listen and CHANGE!

Congratulations on taking the first step to learning, understanding and TAMING men!

CONTENTS

INTRODUCING

A NEW BOOK AND A NEW YOU

You're absolutely right. Something **must** change in your dating life. You're sick of meeting the same kind of guy over and over again. You're sick of falling into one terrible relationship after the next. More importantly, you want to be **in control** of your love life again! What's with all of these loser men that you've been dating? Are good guys really as hard to find as tampons in a Super Wal-Mart? Is it that?

Or is it that you're always being chosen, rather than doing the choosing?

That's a statement you'll be hearing a lot throughout this book. It's going to be the reason for the drastic change that you're about to undertake. It's the starting block that's also the finishing line. You don't "get it" quite yet, but don't worry. I'm going to be your drill sergeant, drilling this point home until it's as natural as breathing.

By the end of this book, you're going to have taken charge of your dating life in a way that catches your friends by surprise and astonishes the hell out of them. Your old social circle will be staring at you with their eyes bulging and their mouths open and **you're** going to say:

"What? You haven't read *The Social Tigress*?"

Stand Tall and Salute Your Drill Sergeant

My name is Gregg, and I'm the author of a handful of Amazon best sellers in the dating genre for both men and women. I fly all over the States, from Las Vegas to Miami to Los Angeles, CA, to teach people my hard-hitting dating techniques.

Girls, if you're single then you NEED this book in combination with my other top Amazon books:

"Who Holds the Cards Now?"
to get a guy to commit and keep him into you.

"Love is in the Mouse"
to expand your reach and land a great man
when time is a factor.

"Committed to Love, Separated by Distance"
to reach a great guy outside your area.

"Power Texting Men" to complete your game.

Guys won't have a prayer if you apply these
POWERFUL BEST SELLERS!

Yep, I'm a genuine "Hitch" if you will; only I'm not as good looking as Will Smith; nor do I need to be. And one of the first lessons I'll be teaching you is that you don't need to be a Victoria Secret model to find true happiness with a guy, either. Oh, *right, right*, you've **heard** that one before, haven't you? But you don't believe it. At least not yet you don't!

I got my start as a dating coach for middle-aged men a while back, but over the years I've noticed that my audience is a bit wider than I first suspected. My website www.singlemiddle-agedguys.com quickly became popular with younger guys (the bastards) and even younger women that were trying to figure out just what the hell was wrong with the guys they kept meeting at the bar scene (there's plenty of potential in that bar, you just don't know how to spot it yet. You've got your "blinders" on. And even if you could, you wouldn't know what to do with it. But I'll get to that in a bit!)

I'm a self-made man, a life-long bachelor, and when it comes to speaking to women, a real "natural" in the art. I live and breathe women, night and day. I love them, cherish them, and would never abuse their trust. Ladies, I want to give you the dating life that you deserve, but only if you get rid of that "all men suck" and "I'll never understand them" mentality.

Put your trust in me for the duration of this book, and I promise that by the end of it you'll never think these thoughts again.

Soldiering On to Becoming a Dating Master

No drill sergeant would be very good at his job if he didn't yell at you to do a few push-ups every now and again. And that's exactly what I'm going to do. Well, metaphorically, that is.

I'm going to be tough on you. I'm going to challenge you to do things you wouldn't normally do. This book will tell you things that your girlfriends will scream are barefaced lies. But I'll tell you what—every single word in here is the truth, and it's going to enable you to call bullshit on the guys that really do suck. That means no more wasted time; it means the end of looking for men in all the wrong places. Quite possibly, it's the end of heartbreak.

Now, if you're damn sick of it all, you can keep sitting there with mascara running down your face, killing a bucket of Rocky Road ice cream with the biggest soup ladle you own...

Or...

You can empower yourself and say "Gregg, I'm **ready** for this. Give it to me straight for the Love of God. I'm sick of pussy-footing around and I'm sick of having my hand held. I want the whole truth and nothing but the truth!"

If that's where you are, then you've come to the right place. If that's not where you are, better look elsewhere for something a little more palatable.

> My book is a shot of whiskey.
> If you want the wine coolers,
> then I'd suggest another bartender.

I'm serving you up cold, hard truth, straight from the blunt, outside perspective of a man who knows the ins and outs of women better than women do!

I'm going on the assumption that you know I'm about to be blunt with you, and that you're completely willing to agree to that because you're sick of taking advice from other women and you get the sinking suspicion that they aren't being totally honest with you. I'm going to tell you right now:

I have no reason to lie to you!

I want you to succeed. More confident women in this world is better for both women AND men! More confident women mean more stable relationships. It means more families stay together in the long run. Hell, it's a Godsend to your Beautiful Unborn Children. The only people it won't benefit are the divorce lawyers because these tips I'm about to show you are not just for the dating scene. They will create the foundation of a long-lasting, sustainable relationship.

Does that sound too good to be true? Well it isn't! This future is in your hands, but you need to take this book seriously. I'm asking you to take it all in from time to time. Remind yourself that you spent money on this book when you could have bought more mascara and more Rocky Road instead.

Why My Book Is Different

Here's some great news: this is the only dating eBook that actually makes it feasible for you to take its methods and get them working for you *immediately*! I'm not kidding—this book was designed to get you moving and shaking. After each chapter is a short list of challenges, some of which you can do on the spot, while others may have to wait until certain conditions are met.

Do these and your life will change **forever**.

No joke, no sales pitch. I'm telling you that straight ahead is more confidence, a stronger social life, and more men. By more men I don't just mean you get to play sex goddess Samantha from Sex & the City in the next movie sequel. It means having a bigger pool to choose the best guy for you. Just like my dating advice for men isn't for slimy pick up artists, my dating advice for women is strictly for those of you that want to explore, date, and eventually find a guy you can settle down with.

Besides, if you're just in it for the sex, why in the world would you pick up a dating book?

Start Your Training Today!

While in theory you could jump through the chapters in the book, I'm strongly recommending you don't. Each chapter builds on the one before it, and if you attempt the challenges in Chapter 7 without having even read the first six chapters, then at best you'll be confused, and at worst you'll make a fool out of yourself at your next outing!

Make this book the last dating book you *ever* buy. That may be bad for my dating book business but if it makes you the confident and beautiful woman that you've always wanted to be, then I will be a happy guy.

With that said, I think we're ready to begin.

Let's make it happen!

CHAPTER 1

A FOUR-STEP PRIMER TO BUILDING CONFIDENCE & ATTRACTING MEN

Before I get into the real meat and potatoes of the book, I wanted to give you ladies my quick four-step process to building the confidence that men drool over. These are hard-hitting facts that will get you going this week, but don't consider it a substitute for skipping the other chapters. It will take some re-programming on your part to get these down pat, so take some time every day, early in the morning or just before bed, and re-read this chapter until you're totally done with the book.

You'll begin implementing these steps in your daily life beginning tomorrow. (Yes, that's an order!)

To put this in the most simple terms possible: men go nuts for girls that have VALUE. Some dating books explain how to demonstrate this to a man. Problem is if you don't have it, as most women don't, you must fake it. And that's where it all goes up in smoke.

Which is why it's time you start acquiring real value. Once you have it you'll be flaunting it to everyone, including the hottest men out there on Saturday nights. By being a woman of value men become the prize, the perk of your investment in yourself. I love how society teaches just the opposite: get the rich guy and you will become a woman of value. It's total bullshit.

So let's jump right into these steps. You'll find each step automatically builds upon the next, and when combined they are a force to be reckoned with.

STEP #1: Find Value by Making Yourself Unique, Live Your Dream

Look around you and you're likely to see a bunch of robots—girls displaying their half-naked bodies to guys, hanging out in packs like wildebeest so guys will never approach, and every single one of them texting away furiously. There is no separation from the next. With that said, how do they ever expect to differentiate themselves long enough to find a good man?

Drill this thought into your head: followers are losers. Only be a follower by choice. Stop following and get motivated. Do your own thing. Dedicate yourself to a new list of activities and get good at them. Brainstorm what your dreams are. Learn to dance, learn to surf. With this a funny thing happens, the seed of self-esteem gets planted and you ATTRACT MEN.

Don't accept things in your life as "this is how it is." Learn to be more open-minded. Hang with a new bunch of friends. Start your own business on the side so you can lose your boss.

What will happen in the eyes of others, men included? They will see you as a risk-taker that is wild and ambitious. This is an instant attraction getter. You see, men become the **benefit** of a woman that has **value**.

So realize your dream and live it. Make it the most important part of your life and watch men suddenly gain interest in you.

STEP #2: Become Aloof

Now that you are following your own dream your time just became very valuable. Men love a girl who is aloof or "not always available". They will tell you the opposite but when you say, "I can't get together because I've got a race on Tuesday." They will want you more.

Once you have defined your dream and are pursuing it, guess what? That guy that you wanted to see just became outdated. You just upgraded yourself by default because you realize that your passion is much more valuable than him. You decide that your choice of men will be different because giving up your time won't just happen with anyone any more. You realize that you will only settle for men that will compliment your life not compromise it. In turn, you become very attractive and desirable.

Guys are driven to women that have limited time because it shows importance. So spend even more of your time pursuing that passion of yours and stay aloof.

Which leads me to my next step...

STEP #3: Gain Status and Become Powerful

You found your dream and you are pursuing it every day along with your other ambitions. Your time is valuable. Start hanging out with others similar to you. They are influential people just like you are becoming. They know their dreams and are living them too.

Next, start teaching others. This makes you powerful in their eyes and your own. Teaching can be done by volunteering time at a soup kitchen or mentoring those less fortunate than you or by training someone that is learning from your rock climbing passion. This adds some wonderful seeds to you confidence jar. Furthermore, when you tell a man that you volunteer, they start thinking "this is a woman that has value and I can see myself dating her long-term".

Weed out the negative people that don't add value to your life. This doesn't mean you have to disrespect them!

Just remain aloof to these people as you do with men. We all have these people in our lives. Hell, some are family members. Give your important time to others that you see as adding value to YOUR life.

Men are attracted to powerful, influential women—or women with status. They are attracted to rock stars and movie stars because they feel they are more important than the average followers in life. You become their status symbol.

STEP #4: Never Shoot for Average

Work out your body harder. Deliver at work better. Respect others who do right by you more often. Argue less and listen more. Help others more. Find your weak links and weld them solid. Every possible feat should have extra gusto behind it. Mindless activities need to be slowly eliminated as they yield negative gain like watching TV and playing video games. How do you feel after watching TV for 3 hours? I feel like a loser.

Again as you pursue your dreams and passions these items fall into place. Confidence builds and you **want** to challenge yourself more. Wake up every day with a catalyst to get you going, mine is music, and live it like it's your last. Say this, "how is this day going to be remembered?" I bet most of your days are the same—so start making them **different**. I love and live by the phrase, "Do something every day that scares you." It's written on my coffee mug!

4 Steps to Attracting Men with Confidence
CONCLUSION

As you become a woman of value positive character traits bloom inside you. You have no need to show off so you listen better. This in turn gains you respect. Jealousy disappears. You now ooze confidence. People count on you in social situations to take control and get everyone involved. Your whole life starts to domino into this character that, six months ago, you would never recognize. This woman is **YOU**.

By following my four steps you will gain confidence day by day. This will take time. But slowly you will be a more confident and a more fulfilled woman. As you find and pursue your own dreams the quality of men you date becomes top notch, which in turn makes you a true woman of value but more importantly, it makes you happy.

This is only the tip of the iceberg when it comes to confidence building. In Chapter 2, we delve into this idea even further, so that by the time you get done, you'll be starting to think like a true social tigress, and your "compromising with men days" will be over for good.

CHAPTER 2

PREPARING A DIFFERENT MINDSET

If you're single, then I've got one thing to say to you:

CONGRATULATIONS!

I can actually imagine you pouting and rolling your eyes after that comment. "Congratulations? Gregg, you jerk, I'm heartbroken and lonely! It's the same thing every day: I get home from work, tell my dog I'm lonely, and have a make-out session with a bag of Hershey's Kisses. You think it's *fun* not having someone around to talk to and go to dinner and a movie with? That's all I want, and you're making fun of me?"

Short answer? Yes. Yes I am. But don't be confused here. I'm not making fun of you in particular. I'm making fun of the fact that you believe so strongly that a man is in charge of your personal happiness.

Now I can see you shaking your head. "No Gregg, I don't believe my happiness is dependent upon a man. I don't *need* a man in my life to make me happy—I just *want* a man in my life to make me happy. There's a difference!"

Is there? The outcome is exactly the same. You're feeling down because you don't have a guy to tag along with. Without a guy, your life is all work and no play. Sure you have a friend or two that you go out to the bars with every Saturday. But the next time you catch yourself pretending to laugh at one of their jokes in order to get that hot guy's attention over by the pool tables, just remember Ol' Gregg said "I told you so!"

And it's not just the bars, either. During a movie with your girlfriends, you can't help but wish Prince Charming was sitting there beside you instead, holding your hand during that gushy romance scene. Using the Stairmaster at that busy gym works out your eyes more than it does your butt. Put your hand up if you're guilty of any of this. It's okay, it's just me here.

I've got a straightforward question that I want you to answer as honestly as you can: Do you believe that a man is necessary to make your life purposeful?

Maybe yes, maybe no, maybe not sure? Well, I'm certain that within 30 seconds of talking to you, I'd know the answer. Want to know how I'd figure it out so quickly? Take your best guess. I'll tell you in just a bit.

The Makings of a Woman of Value

I wanted to congratulate you for a reason, and by the end of this chapter I want you to be congratulating yourself as well. Being single is an **amazing** experience! For one, it's a time for taking care of you and you alone. See old friends and visit the family. Do things you've always wanted to do—things that you don't have time for when a guy is around.

It's also an **adventure**! I want you to get excited about what's out there and embracing your newfound freedom. I know, I know, maybe that freedom doesn't look all that appealing right now. But we are going to change that over the course of this book.

Lastly, and most important, this is your chance, maybe your last chance ever, of developing a life of value, a life of value that is entirely YOURS, outside of a relationship. This has huge implications for your self-esteem, your dating life and your future relationships. It is extremely rare to see women (and men, for that matter) make these drastic changes in a relationship. In almost every case, the seeds must be planted when you are **single**.

Don't shortchange yourself.

Think about what I just said. Rarely do we take major risks or change course when we are dating someone. Our **personal** growth in a way becomes stunted, because relationship stability demands that we don't *get out there* and *do* things that are scary, crazy, and above all, rich in fresh new experiences. Introduce kids and forget about traveling to new places. Start your own business? Can't do it, it's too risky.

Yes, you can grow as a couple, and yes, you can better yourself in a relationship. But real, personal growth where you tempt the bounds of what you can and cannot do...that's singles stuff, risk-taker stuff. In relationships, people become risk-averse. People want safety and comfort. The last thing they want to do is tear things down.

In your 20's and even 30's you're growing immensely. If you get bogged down with a loser guy your personal growth literally stagnates. Before you know it, it's too late and they have wasted years because you didn't learn to fly, aka, learn to become a **woman of value.**

Learn to fly, then meet a guy.

If not, some loser will mold you into a clay sculpture that is NOT you. Good friends of mine have been destroyed by this kind of life. One particular friend met her husband in high school. They were recently divorced. She has no idea what to do with herself outside of the relationship. She is LOST.

He was her **hobby**, something I will teach you to never, ever, do. Don't let this happen to you!

I listened to a girl recently that complained all her friends were married or in relationships. They were all very young, and so was she for that matter. I told her the truth, which is that many of these relationships will end and her friends will not have the skills to meet decent, good men because they were never developed. Young women that have survived and prospered when they were single have developed the skills to be happy on their own...a guy is just the whip cream and cherry on top!

This isn't to say you can't grow with a guy. You can. But it needs to be the RIGHT guy. And this guy can only be picked by a high value woman that lives a life of abundance and not scarcity. A passive, low self-esteem woman may get herself an unmotivated soon to be overweight couch potato.

This book will not allow that to happen to you.

So that's why I need you to take a step back and embrace your singleness for AT LEAST a month. During this time you'll work on a different mindset where you'll need to brainstorm your passions and pursue them.

And what happens? Funny thing—along comes a high quality guy with similar passions that you can GROW with and be HAPPY. A guy who's motivated, cares about his body, takes on a new business with you and travels the world with you and the kids!

Chapter 2 is about developing a confident mindset which, bluntly speaking, you're 100% positively screwed without. The odds of you making an **independent** and **educated** choice regarding whom to date without this mindset, and thus the odds of you finding a relationship that will last a lifetime, are so stacked against you that you'd have a better chance of being struck by lightning. You leave whom you meet up to luck and blind chance. And this gives the bar sharks, jerks and pick-up artists an opening to swoop in and make your life hell. Why? Because you let yourself be chosen, rather than make a choice on your own.

Giving chance the finger

Really, really think about this: of all the things in your life, of ALL the things, why would you leave the person that you spend your entire life with to chance? This is the single most important decision you will ever make, and yet you're perfectly ready to let some guy with a pretty face and a smattering of charm give you his number and then wine you and dine you.

Ladies, you're smarter than this. Lots of guys know how you want to be treated, and they will use it to their advantage to try to get you in the sack. It isn't good enough that he gave you roses, paid for your California Roll and opened the door for you.

Hell, most of you are willing to spend more time considering which color eyeliner looks good with your base than you do making logical (yes, logical!) choices concerning a man.

We're changing this, and we're doing it *right now!*

Love shouldn't be a rush job, and neither should dating. The most obvious way of sabotaging your happiness with a man is to go about the process like you're in a hurry. You don't need to be in a hurry! Whether you're lonely, your biological clock is ticking away, or all of your friends have abandoned you for husbands and boyfriends, you need to keep your chin up and say:

> "I'm finding a guy on my terms, and I'll find him when I'm ready to find him, not when my emotions, my hormones, or my friends tell me I should."

CUTTING THE CRAP:
4 Myths Women Believe That Demand Debunking

We're going to continue building up this new mindset, but before we do, a few unfounded claims concerning men and dating need to be thoroughly washed out of your head for good, because they are only holding you back. These lies are very persistent, and they will stop a woman from ever finding the confidence she needs to make this new, empowering mindset work for her. So when you hear whispers in your head giving credence to the crap below, it's your job to get the duct tape out and shut them up!

Myth #1:
The "men only want the hottest chicks" myth

A common misconception, spewed out by magazines like Cosmo that swear they love all women, but really only market a single, static image of what a woman should be in **their eyes**. You all know this, ladies, yet you buy the lie. The truth is most women can't hope to attain that ideal image, and nor should you want to. Because at the end of the day, *it's not important to the guys that matter.*

I'm being realistic here, not optimistic. The guys that you'd ideally be looking for, the ones that you would actually be happy with, do not absolutely have to have the hottest chick they can get their hands on. The problem is that this is the kind of woman that we ogle over whenever we are out and about, and so you assume that's all we want. In reality, while we enjoy looking, we don't necessarily believe that to be the best thing for us. Stability and love rank higher on our lists than looks do, at least in the long run.

Given, if you're 300 pounds and you have a set of horse teeth, it may be a bit more difficult to get your foot in the door, **especially** if you're only looking in the bars. But the tricks I'm going to teach you will ensure that even those that weren't endowed with a single attractive feature on the outside can find a partner that loves them. These tricks will highlight the qualities that men find attractive no matter what the woman looks like.

As far as fashionable clothes and shoes go, while it's a plus to nab a girl that knows how to dress, it can also be a nightmare for guys as they watch their bank accounts dwindle and their closets explode with women's shoes. Ladies, you get hung up about the idea that with that pair of new shoes you'll be bagging guys all over the place. But I've got news for you: **Guys barely notice your shoes!**

We wouldn't know if that's real anaconda you're sporting or spray-painted cowhide. Our collective minds cannot fathom the distinctions between Manolo, Ferragamo and Gucci. If you have a closet of 100 different pairs of shoes, we won't be excited, we'll be terrified! If David Beckham wasn't making millions of dollars a year, he would be so stressed over what his wife was buying he would lose his mind. Because most of the guys you'll be dating aren't likely to be millionaires, they probably don't care how well your diamond-encrusted laces match your tank top, and they will be more than happy if you keep your shoes to five pairs or less.

Remember: don't buy the lie! Your appearance is only an excuse for not stepping out there. When it comes to women of true value, beauty is a secondary consideration.

Did you know that in ancient Rome men found fat women more attractive than skinny ones?

In Africa, men go ape-shit wild over women who have stretched their necks to twice their normal size.

Beauty will always be in the eye of the beholder.

Myth #2:
The "I'm not outgoing enough to find a guy" myth

If you don't think you're outgoing with men, it's because you aren't in your element. Are you not outgoing when you are with your best friends? Your parents? Your siblings? I do not doubt that you may be nervous around new men, but at the end of the day, is being shy one of your defining characteristics? If I were to guess, I'd say probably not. You *are* outgoing, you just aren't outgoing in your dating life.

This myth often comes up because women interact with men in very general settings, settings that are often busy and not intimate, leading them to assume they are too shy to ever meet guys. That means you're potentially meeting them at bars, on college campuses, in grocery stores, etc. Within these general locations, you have almost no substance to start up a conversation with ("So, uh, those organic tomatoes look pretty ripe today, uh, don't you think?") You have no good reason to believe you're shy in general just because you're shy in these situations. In reality, these situations **suck** when it comes to finding men.

Drop the general locations and the general chitchat, and suddenly you're the most outgoing person in the world. To find that substance, you need to get specific. Find something you love to do and learn everything you can about it. Then join groups that have a similar interest. I'll be getting into this in more detail later on, but trust me when I say that this **works**! It makes a world of difference talking to a guy when you both are on equal footing and enjoy discussing the topic at hand.

Don't worry if you can't think of any groups you would join or passions that you want to learn about. This takes time, and I'll be helping you develop these passions later in Chapter 2.

Myth #3:
The "I believe in fate" myth

This may be the most destructive myth that stops women from finding their perfect match. The single most important thing you need to remember is that your dating life is in **your** control. When you allow "fate" to take the wheel, you've mentally allowed yourself to take that back seat in your own life, putting you in a situation where you are no longer choosing men, but being chosen by them.

Don't let this happen! The reason we allow these kinds of thoughts into our heads is because they make us feel better. They take away some of the stress that comes with making everyday decisions, as much in our regular lives as in our dating lives. The truth however is that fate is only masquerading as a feel-good fix to your problems, when in reality you have a much better chance of finding that perfect guy on your own!

Fate may exist, or it may not. But why take the chance? What if we all just waited around for fate to do something for us? We would be a world of followers. By being proactive and taking control, really taking control, is going to give you a better shot at finding great men and forming a great relationship with that man.

You're in control of your dating life, and neither person nor deity can take that away from you. Starting today, it's time for **you** to take fate into your own hands!

Myth #4:
The "all men suck" myth

It's only during your darkest moments that you dig this little myth out of the closet, but oh how useful it is! Ladies, you're pretty quick to let this little voice comfort you after a terrible breakup or a run in with your classic pick-up artist at the local bar. But if you let it soothe you for too long, it will wreak some serious dark and sinister magic on your brain. Stereotyping in general is a bad habit, but doing so with men could keep you from finding a really great guy to spend your life with.

In all likelihood you've been meeting guys in all the wrong places, or rather, you keep allowing men to choose you, rather than you choosing them. If this is the case, it's no wonder that your view of men is so distorted: you're just meeting the same idiot guy over and over again! And why would this be? Because you're allowing yourself to be chosen.

Listen, if you're reading this book, chances are you have dated some real jerks in the past, and every now and again you can hear a little voice telling you that we are all terrible and not even to bother. Don't listen to it! You can get angry, you can tell your friends how much we suck, but at the end of the day, don't let it keep you from meeting more guys. I promise that, over the course of this book, you will learn where to meet descent men, and how to filter out the duds.

Plenty more myths where that came from!

Other myths exist, and when they come up over the course of the book I will immediately show them as what they are: excuses, fears, nerves, laziness, and whatever else that could stop you from taking this mindset and taking charge of your life in entirely new ways. At the end of the day, you need to be able to identify these as myths and keep them from influencing your dating life. Only then can I guarantee that you will develop the mindset you need to have the best dating life possible.

The Ultimate Key to Dating and
Finding the Relationship of Your Dreams

While dating, you're trying to find a **healthy** relationship, not just **any** relationship. You don't want to find just anybody. You want someone that is good for *you*, and in order to do that you need to *know* you. And that's what a lot of this book is all about!

Do you remember a few pages up when I told you that I would know within 30 seconds of talking to you whether or not a man was the primary source of purpose in your life? Well, I'd find out the answer to that little question by asking you about your social life. Why? Because having a strong, developed social life is the key to a great dating life. It's also the key to a confident woman. Finally, it's the key to keeping the passion alive once you make that transition into a serious relationship. To sum it up, your social life is **everything!**

Don't get me wrong. Your confidence as a woman also has roots in other areas of your life, such as your family, your job, and your education. But these things are *not* a social life, not by any means. A social life takes into account your interests, and developing your interests with others who share them will become the nucleus of your independence and pride.

This is such a critical aspect in the book, I have devoted an entire chapter on how to develop and maintain your new interests and a new social life, one that is as far removed from the bar scene. Now, I don't mean you should stop going to bars. Bars are a great way to supplement your social life. But they should only be a supplement, and not the entire thing! Remember that your social life is more than just about meeting guys, it's about developing personal pride and confidence. It's about developing **you** in a way that is totally different from anyone else.

A social life is about confidence. You are empowered when you have things to do outside of the work scene and the dating scene. You feel better about yourself because you're *growing*. And that growth is critical to sustaining your new mindset, promoting greater self-awareness and more self-esteem than you could ever imagine—think happy endorphins dancing in your head!

How will this help you later? You will choose a partner that will grow with you, not one that will be stagnant on the couch. You see: by defining yourself first, you will pick the proper man by default later.

Now to Get This New Mindset Working For You!

It's one thing to just sit on this knowledge; it's another thing entirely to start taking control and *acting*. And that's exactly what we're aiming to do in Chapter 2. We're going to take the new you and we're going to apply it to the beginnings of your new dating life.

By the time we finish, you'll be a brand name—a recognizable, unique woman with tons of value to offer. A social tigress that is free to roam and find men on **her** terms!

Challenges for Chapter 2:

In Chapter 2 my goal was to get you EXCITED about a new approach to dating and a new, confident you. Starting from Chapter 2, I'm going to be jotting down a number of challenges that will test your commitment to the new you in every way. While these may be easy now, they will get progressively harder as we move forward. So be prepared!

Challenge:

Jot down 10 advantages of being single. This is to calm and prepare you for a month or two of concentrating on yourself and not meeting a man.

Challenge:

Explore some potential hobbies.
Go to http://www.stormthecastle.com/the-list-of-hobbies.htm

Challenge:

Go back over the myths in this chapter and try to think of a time when you actually believed them.

Challenge:

Google "activities for singles" plus the city where you live, and browse what comes up. (Extra credit if you check out "Events and Adventures".)

Challenge:

In the old days a woman would drop her handkerchief at the feet of a handsome man. Use a modern version of this little trick to your advantage. At school, work or anywhere public for that matter, drop something on purpose while you're next to a good looking guy. (No this isn't silly! You're in training!)

CHAPTER 3

BABES WITH BRAND NAMES

Marketing and Dating?
They're Practically Synonymous!

No, I didn't just rip out a chapter from a random Marketing 101 textbook to use in my dating guide—but if I *had*, it would have fit perfectly into chapter three. Believe it or not, marketing and dating have a lot in common. Everything that makes for a good marketing campaign makes for a good dating campaign: targeting a specific demographic, creating a unique brand that people recognize, and marketing your product in the right places (this is the only time I'll call you a product, I swear). All of this is smart marketing—and smart dating.

In this chapter we apply these very marketing techniques to dating. My goal here is to get you thinking about how you are a complete unique offering, a 100% bona fide original.

You have interests and passions and goals that, when combined together, make up a very distinctive personality and character. Now, you may not be able to see that character yet, but I guarantee it exists. You just haven't looked hard enough for it yet!

Developing your interests isn't something you can do in days or even weeks. We're talking months here—**years** perhaps. You have to be in it for the long haul, or you'll be aiming for a life where boys and boys alone are your sole purpose and only hobby. And that, ladies, is more than just a boring sales pitch: it's faulty merchandise, made in a dirty sweatshop in China.

Why a unique brand makes all the difference

A unique brand is the core of any successful business or person. When I say brand, I don't just mean a familiar icon like McDonald's golden arches or Playboy's bunny. A brand is a personality of sorts, it's a feeling you get when you walk into a certain restaurant or purchase a line of clothing. A brand can be obvious or subtle. It can be classic and elegant or bold and rebellious. For companies, and in other cases for individuals, their brand ends up defining who they are, and who buys whatever it is they're offering.

Just like how smart branding can boost the revenue for companies and increase the clout for individuals, bad branding, or no branding at all, is disastrous. Without that particular brand, you will have no way of differentiating yourself from your competitors, which, when it comes to dating, means other women.

When you try to compete with other women in the dating game without your own particular brand, you end up with one defining characteristic: how slutty can I get? How much sex can I have on display for the boys? That is **not** the way to find success in your dating life...

And the only way you'll be able to avoid it is by finding your own, distinctive brand.

Kim Kardashian...role model for women everywhere?

Being hot does not guarantee you'll go viral. Is Kim Kardashian the hottest chick in the world? Hell no. And yet she rules the airwaves for entertainment news. On the *Forbes* 100 Most Influential Persons list for 2013, she comes in as number 66 (her TV rank is 15). In a facial recognition poll during the 2013 New York gubernatorial race, she was the only one that scored a 75% recognition rate. No politician could come close to being as recognizable as she is. In fact, just one politician received a facial recognition above 50%!

And why is she famous? Did she rescue baby seals? Did she save African children? Does she make a mean tuna casserole? If fame was directly correlated with publishing naked pictures on the internet, I expect Kim's fame would be a bit crowded out. Instead she dominates.

Kim is the perfect example of a branding success. She combined a personality that was bitchy, impulsive and unsentimental, and added to it a laundry list of interests including singing, acting, hairstyling, selling things on eBay, and playing entrepreneur with a closet organizing business she started. She was intensely pursuing her goals up to and after she got noticed holding hands with Nick Lachey, who in turn was more famous for dating Jessica Simpson than for being in 98 Degrees. (I'm sure I have Nick Lachey fans scoffing at me for saying that, but I'm sticking to it!)

Nothing she did should have made her successful outright. Her beauty alone, or her money alone, or her family's connections alone, is not enough to secure her the fame she has now—which leads us to believe something else is going on here. That something of course is who she is, her personal brand, a mixture of both personality, ambition, and interests, all coming together to incite massive amounts of intrigue.

As much as you may not like her, she could not have gotten to where she is now without dedication to her interests and goals. I mean, Paris Hilton hangs out with plenty of hot sluts. Why was Kim the only one that exploded into fame?

And **that**, ladies, is why I'm calling her the role model that you need to keep in mind in this chapter and beyond. Love her or hate her, she could just as easily have wallowed outside of the spotlight forever if not for her ambitions, interests and personality.

How to approach your brand

You've got a seven day routine that you keep to. Maybe you're busy, maybe you think you've got too much time on your hands. In either case, you can take **two hours** a week to pursue a hobby. Really consider what two hours is to a seven day schedule. You have 168 hours to play with during any given week. Don't tell me you can't pursue a new interest for two hours out of that 168.

Maybe photography interests you. Grab a cheap camera, hit up a class and **meet** people. You could hate it! But you might very well love it. If it's a passion, wouldn't you want to know? Besides, even if it's a dead end, you got out there and grew from your new experiences. You have stories to tell. You have done it once and you know you can do it again. And even more important, you have newfound **confidence** that will improve every aspect of your life.

Now go for a firearms permit. Motorcycle license. Surf. Take yoga classes. Live anywhere near ski resorts? Take snowboard lessons. Eventually a passion will stick, or a person will make an impression on you, so much so that you want to keep them in your life. This is how we grow, and it is eventually how we meet quality men.

Do not choose a man as your passion.
Instead, choose a passion and let it lead you to a man.

Plagiarize at your own risk

Another tried and true fact about marketing is that trying to copy someone else's brand is a recipe for disaster. If you intend to become Pink's doppelganger I guarantee you will not enjoy the same success that she has had. You can **base** your style after them, but if you try to match them entirely you'll look like a fool. In marketing and dating, plagiarizing just doesn't work.

This is a God-honest truth about marketing: no company has ever found incredible success by copying another company's brand "word for word". Sure they can take ideas from them, or share a similar set of goals, but the reality is you can't replicate success. It's only through being unique that you can break through and make your presence known.

Find inspiration from others, but never, ever copy someone else's style, no matter how successful it was for them.

It's raining men! Halleluiah!

Outside of being a catchy tune, It's Raining Men by The Weather Girls wouldn't be as full of Halleluiahs as you may think if it really happened. One of the most important rules of marketing is that you never want to cast your net too wide. If you start marketing a product to the entire population, you're not likely to be successful, mainly because your marketing efforts are **too general**.

To combat this, marketers learn the demographics that are more likely to buy a product, and then they market specifically to that demographic. And just like a marketer, if you don't target a certain demographic of men, you'll be finding too many guys, instead of the right **kind** of guy **for you**.

> The more you learn about yourself, the more you find out about what kind of MAN you want. Right now, what would you say if I asked you what kind of man you were looking for? Someone nice? Someone handsome? Someone that treats you with respect? Someone who doesn't cheat on you? This is all good and fine, but it's also extremely general.

You don't want a wider selection—you want a more refined one!

If you're marketing to everyone, you're marketing to no one. It's the same thing with dating. If you're throwing yourself into the faceless club and bar scene, where the only distinctions come from how much you can drink and how high you can hike your skirt up, then you're not honing your demographic enough.

That said I want you to keep an open mind about what your demographic is. Women tell me what they **think** they want in a man. I ask who they date and it's usually the same type of guy over and over. I'll ask them why they don't try dating men that are older, younger, or a completely different character or race. With this question, I usually get a generic response like "Oh I don't date older guys" or "I only date Jewish men who are college grads." Usually they have no **real** reason why they don't want to try dating someone different.

Expand your horizons, cast your net overboard and let some unusual fish enter your dating net...Hell, they may taste good!

Developing Your Personal Brand

How strong your brand is will depend on how much you put into it. If you barely give it any thought, or if you simply continue to ignore potential interests, you'll likely have little or no brand at all and thus no real defining characteristics outside of general appearance and personality traits.

But if you make it a point to really hone in on what makes you special, and if you focus on how you can build upon the personality you have, you'll quickly find that your self-worth—and at the same time the value of your brand—will increase exponentially. If you're willing to work for it, then I'm willing to help you get there.

Plotting the course

What defines you? Where do you go? What do you like? What traits impress you that you wish you had? Who is your idol? Why? When were last really happy? What was it that made you that happy? What can you do to stay happy? What do you stand for? Why are you asking me all of these questions?

I want you to answer this tough question; "How would I define myself?"

Questions, my dear, are everything. Nothing would get done without them. Therefore, once you've made a decision to become a woman of value, your first task is to start asking yourself a lot of **deep** questions.

Ask questions that explore you. I'll bet you have never asked the questions above. Many of the answers you may not like but that's OK. The answers give you a baseline to start thinking about the upcoming changes. Some questions are easier to answer than others. The answer to "What's my life's passion?" may be easy for some to answer, and impossible (at the moment, at least) for others.

I'm assuming a lot of you out there have thought about this. You would love to have things to do outside of work or school, but you have no idea what. Even worse, you may be under the assumption that you're weird because you don't have a passion or an interest. If this is you, drop the thought. It's normal not to know what your passion is.

What passions are not

Unless you get extremely lucky, your passion is not something you'll just happen to come across randomly. Passions aren't just sitting in your head, waiting impatiently for you to take them up. For example, maybe playing the violin could incite a passion in you for playing it. But unless you make the attempt, you'll never know.

And that's the problem: most of us have to **work** to find our passions. If it was so damn easy, most of us would be pursuing them, and I wouldn't be writing this at all.

As I said, some people get luckier than others when looking around for their passions. For instance, I wasn't always a dating coach, nor did the thought really cross my mind until a friend of mine told me I should start up a website. One thing led to another, and now I'm happily engaged with writing these books and helping men and women find dating confidence. I've always loved the art of dating, but did I ever think it would turn out like this? No way!

Passions are really just pastimes that engage us and make us happy. You want to find something that **challenges** you and **helps you grow**. Something that's just fun won't do that.

> Most people will lie on their death bed
> having never pursued or even found their passion.

Don't get depressed if you try something out and then don't feel motivated to do it again. It may take a lot of different tries to find things that interest you. Your job right now is to get **motivated** to find the thing that **challenges** you!

So, Gregg, how do I *find* said interests, anyway?

Finding your interests will take some effort, but luckily there are a lot of men and women that are looking at the same time you are. In fact, it has never been easier to use the internet as a platform to find people with similar interests. Or, if you aren't sure what might interest you, the internet is a great place to get ideas.

If you're worried that you're too shy to be a part of any new group, then I've got two words for you: **Man Up**. You may not be confident yet, but gaining confidence is all about *putting yourself out there!* Listen, are you in this just to read dating book after dating book and not follow through, or do you want to make **real** changes? I expect you want real changes, and that begins by meeting new people and going out of your comfort zone.

One crucial thing to consider when looking for interests to pursue is to not become overwhelmed by doing everything at once. You have all the time **in the world** to work on this! It's a never-ending process of searching for interests and improving upon them, so don't think you have to be Speedy Gonzalez...just keep things simple and don't overwhelm yourself.

This is the biggest problem that people have when they start looking for their interests: they take too much in all at once and give up because they spend too much time daydreaming about the end result.

The problem with that thinking is that there is no end result! This is a change in mindset: you're seeking out and

pursuing interests to develop a happier, more valuable life. There is no end to this—it's a lifelong pursuit.

Developing your personal brand means you have to start getting out there and making it happen. Yes you can write lists of things that could potentially interest you, but if that's all you do, you'll go nowhere. Ladies, you need to **look** for ideas. They don't just plop into your head like magic!

The more you go in search of ideas, and the more you start pursuing interests, the more confidence you build, and the easier it is. Once you build up that confidence, you're true personality traits will start shining through stronger than ever before. Remember: personality is a big part of your brand too. But personality isn't always easy to express when you're shy or uncomfortable. More confidence means you display that personality stronger than ever.

Here's an example for you: Last year, I met a girl named Jen who was very sweet and shy. As I got to know her I could see she had a wilder side and had an interest in my motorcycle. As motorcycles seem to carry that "I'm wild and free" image, I told her to learn how to ride a bike. She resisted at first but then followed through. Fast forward to today and now Jen owns a bike and has met some new friends, one of whom is her boyfriend. Her brand is not sweet and shy anymore—it's outgoing and rebellious. But she would have never figured it out if she didn't "stir the pot" as I state in *The Social Tigress*.

What might've happened to Jen? Some dominate guy could have entered her life and molded her into something she's not because she was clueless about what she stood for. This sweet and shy girl would not have had the chance to discover who she really was and what she really enjoyed in life. This is how relationships fail; this is why people stumble through life unhappy.

Why All of This Matters to Your Dating Life

Being able to fall back on your interests and passions is going to save you a lot of heartbreak in the future. Women who don't have passions either go straight into another bad relationship, or dig their heels into their careers and leave the dating game, potentially forever. Neither one of these scenarios is a good thing. They are preventable with solid interests because you can get your mind **off of men** when the worst happens.

And as I mentioned above, having hobbies when you're dating is an incredible way of keeping the things interesting, and this is even truer when it becomes a relationship. You can really throw a man off when you have an active social life. Men **love it** when their women have a developed social life that doesn't revolve around them. Furthermore, you will avoid the "jealous types" who want their partner at home and not part of any social circle.

With an outside social life, you're not predictable—and that is the key to a strong relationship.

Concluding the Chapter

If you got anything out of this chapter, I hope it's that you are a true believer in the art of branding yourself. When women develop distinct brands that they are proud of, everything in their lives realign, not least of which is the kind of men they meet in the dating scene.

Women with brands have more control over their lives and a stronger appreciation for who they are. They also have stronger relationships that are more capable of surviving over time. What kind of woman you are determines what kind of man is good for you. The less you know yourself the less likely it is that you will make an informed decision about finding the right guy FOR YOU.

And just like everything else that has this much incredible value to it...it's impossible to develop overnight. Take your time, start seeking out potential interests, and when overwhelmed, stop thinking about it! Take it back up the next day if you have to, but never stop searching until you find something, and when you do, never stop challenging yourself. Because when you have nothing to challenge you, you can't expect to grow.

Challenges for Chapter 3:

Challenge:
Start branding yourself by listing 25 positive characteristics: I am charming, witty, bold, I listen well, I look great in skirts.

Challenge:
Answer this question; what defines me? I bet you don't know the answer today, that's OK. Keep asking until you FIND the answer.

Challenge:
List 10-20 potential hobbies (from the challenge in Chapter 2) that interest you; Surfing, ball room dancing, chefs class, endurance races, pottery class, writing courses so I can write Amazon books. Now pick 1 and make it happen.

Challenge:
On the internet, sign up for one women's group and one single's group in your area. Afterward, look to see what kind of activities they are doing.

Challenge:
Go onto www.Wordle.net and create your very own word cloud.

Challenge:
Go onto the website of a college near you and download a PDF file of their class catalog. Scroll down and highlight any classes that sound interesting. Now, start looking on the internet for groups that offer similar activities.

Challenge:
Ideas, ideas, and more ideas! Ask five people you know what they do for fun outside of work.

CHAPTER 4

SO THIS GIRL WALKS INTO A BAR...

The Queen of the Bar Scene

What kind of dating book would be complete without a dedicated chapter on meeting men at bars? Chapter Four is important because plenty of women like the bar scene regardless of whether they have things to do outside of it or not. And that's just fine! Hell, there have been times in my life where I practically *lived* in bars.

They can be a lot of fun, but make no mistake: **bars are shark tanks, and they're (for the most part) crappy places to meet men.**

They are full of predators that don't want to date you or even know you more than a few hours (ideally it would be minutes). They want one thing and one thing only. And while it goes without mentioning, they're damn good at it, too. I mean, they are *careerists*. Imagine having a 40-hour workweek trying to have sex with women. They know exactly what you want to hear, and they know exactly how you want to be treated. They are masters, professionals, ARTISTS in the trade.

You'll meet them. You may even have an enjoyable night or two with them. But they won't date you. They won't meet your parents. They'll say they like your cat when they don't. And then one day, he will stop calling you and not return your texts. Even though you had a feeling, a hunch, it will still hurt like hell. Because you've been used, and that sucks for any-one. Ladies, do this enough times and you'll be literally **dying** for a decent man.

"Well thanks Gregg, for pissing on my Saturday nights!" Hey, I wouldn't be doing my job if I didn't warn you about them. And besides, you probably already knew. The question isn't if they're there, the question is how to spot them and avoid them. Then, I'll help you track down the guys that are **worth** dating.

But before we get to any of that, there are some critical tips that I want to share with you regarding both your appear-ance and your interaction with men at the bars. I want to get you making not just any impression, but the **right** im-pression with the **right** kind of guy. Think about it as styling tips from a guy's perspective. And not just any guy—but the guy who has seen every conceivable kind of woman in every type of crazy, elegant, slutty outfit imaginable.

I'm going to explain what men are thinking when they see you walking into the bar. So stay tuned. You might learn something!

Stepping Up Your Game

Time to take your new confidence and step it up a notch, each and every one of you! You aren't the same woman you were before you started this book. You've made some changes, you're pursuing your passions and men are show-ing up at your new venues and not just the bars. You're new and improved. Now let's apply what we've learned to the bar scene and get my methods **working for you!**

But I'm not valuable yet!

"Gregg, you're moving too fast! I don't feel confident enough yet. I haven't found my passion yet! How can I be a woman of value and meet good guys if I haven't had time to figure this all out?"

Remember when I said that finding your passion would take a lot of time? The goal is to go out and *pursue* things that *could* be your passion, which in turn builds your self-es-teem. **When you get out of the house and start looking for things that interest you, you're already there. You've already become a woman of value.** That's it! *You can get better* but that's all there is to it. So am I really moving too fast? Absolutely not! Take care of those challenges in the last two chapters and then full speed ahead!

Who do you want to impress with that first impression?

First impressions are just as important as you think they are. But without even realizing it you could wind up impressing the wrong kind of guy.

I've seen it before: women with great bodies but zero self-confidence rely on pure sex appeal to get noticed. They come in wearing whatever they can to get men lusting after them. Skirts that are so short there're practically half-mooning them, or pants so tight they're cutting off circulation to their camel toe. To top it all off they wear 6-inch heels, turning themselves into a statuesque pedestal of sex.

Even if you're not so bold, the reality is you don't have to get even close to this to make a good first impression. First impressions are more in how you're acting, how you're smiling, what you're **doing** more than they are your appearance.

Now don't go around telling everyone that I said you have to dress conservative at the bar scene! But style and sex are two totally different things, and while I won't be there to pick things out of your closet for you, I can at least explain the general idea to you. Style is closer to confidence then it is to what you're wearing. It's clothing you feel comfortable in, that you feel **sexy** in, without seeming to give you away all at once.

This is important: you're going for subtlety. You're going for intrigue. You're going for bangs over one eye, a coy smile, and a strut that says you know exactly where you're going. Note that I mentioned nothing that had to do with your clothes. Find clothes that accent your best features, but do yourself a favor and don't make it look like you're selling body parts at a local garage sale.

Get men **wondering** about what you've got in there. You'd be surprised at how little it takes to get our minds wandering! By dressing a bit more subtle than a "bar girl" you stand out.

Men have two mindsets when they go out; girls they can fuck tonight and women that they can settle down with. By dressing too slutty a man's brain is quickly triggered to having sex without an emotional connection that is needed in a lasting relationship. Don't let this happen. Impress a man with your style, wit and uniqueness, and not just your legs, boobs and ass.

It's not that we don't notice the hottie wearing stilettos showing her thong (because we sure as hell do) it's that it quickly turns her into something with only one use. If you're dressed like that, we have a pretty good idea what you're after even if it's nothing more than attention. And believe it or not, most decent guys will leave you to the sharks.

It's your choice if you're looking for something more. Stop thinking all looks and start believing in the power of **subtlety** and **style**.

You Know the Rules, So Let's Get to Work!

You know what you need to do? You need to take Gregg's **SOLO CHALLENGE**.

"OMG what? I have to go out alone? Gregg, now I KNOW you're crazy!" Ah yes, whenever I tell a woman to take my solo challenge, she's stunned. Going out alone is a big step. But it will do **wonders** for your confidence and your ability to talk to men. Talking to men is just like anything else: after a while it becomes second nature. But you have to try to get to that point. And my Solo Challenge is your one-way ticket to get there and desensitize yourself from any fear you feel. This way when that handsome man shows up you will act the very same way you act around anyone else and that is relaxed and confident!

To complete the solo challenge and earn your place in Gregg's Solo Challenge Hall of Fame, you must perform a number of key tasks, not least of which is finding an appropriate bar. This particular bar:

- Should be packed with people, but not so packed that its standing room only.

- Would ideally have a large round bar in the center of the room, so you can see the people sitting across from you (for easier access to guys.)

- Is a place you know and feel comfortable in, but also somewhere that you are confident that you won't run into anyone familiar.

- Preferably has TVs that you can look at. Why TV? Because it isn't a good idea to be staring off into nothing!

It's going to be tempting as hell,
but keep the phone away!

Guys won't want to come up to you
if you're typing out a text to one of your friends.

For the Solo Challenge, you must also ALWAYS have in mind:

- That you are supposed to be there. You don't belong anywhere else in the world. You came to have a drink and hang out.

- That you need to keep an open posture. Think: relaxed and inviting.

- You have NO competition because there is not a girl in the room choosing a guy like you are doing.

And when the men come up (and they will) you'll only get a passing grade from Gregg Himself if you:

- Maintain your confidence. **He** is the one going out on a limb here. **You're** just relaxing and doing your thing. Answer his questions. Ask questions of your own. Root for him!

- Throw him off a bit. That means saying no to his drink offer, while at the same time making it known that you don't mind him being there.

- Don't make any commitments to him. Say something unexpected. If you like him, give him your number and tell him you'll be back next week – then leave. If he gets annoying, clam up and give him the cold shoulder until he leaves.

Do all these things, and you have successfully earned a place in the Solo Challenge Hall of Fame. That is definitely reason enough to be proud! Think about it: how many women would do what you just did?

Take the Solo Challenge Extreme Edition outside the bar scene

This time around you'll need a different venue, something like a like wine tasting or some type of charity event where the sharks don't swim (as much). Only in this instance, the Solo Challenge Extreme Edition requires that **you** make the move. Pick a man, close the distance and make an excuse to engage.

Ask him a question, make an observation, tell a joke or give him a challenge. "Should I try the white zinfandel or the pinot?" "Hey what do you think of that girl's blouse?" "I dare you to cut in line and grab me a margarita...and get yourself one too, my treat." "Hey tell me if you think this is funny...'there were these two guys...'"

Any of these lines work well. Men want attention, and that handsome young fellow will be stunned and supremely grateful that **you** came up to **him**. Don't forget: men **love** helping women. And most important, they **need** to feel worthy. You supply this and you end up helping yourself at the same time.

Afraid to take the complete Solo Challenge? Warm up to it!

Do this: have your friend(s) meet you one hour later. This way you can still feel safe knowing you will be joined, but in the meantime you get some "man meeting" practice in. You can also go out earlier than usual with your friends and get all the girly news out of the way. Then make a pact to MEET guys. Stir the pot and go in.

Don't try this with friends dedicated to their boyfriends or husbands. You can see them some other time. Right now this is **you** time. You need the practice meeting good guys. They don't. If they are slowing you down, it isn't rude to share a practice night with your single friends.

Why going solo works

Guys are as intimidated of you as you are of them. The dateable ones are more likely to come up to you if you're alone. Then again, the bad ones will make moves also. But this is where you can practice spotting the differences between the two.

This also gives you a chance to feel comfortable with yourself **without** someone that you know right beside you. Having a drink at a bar by yourself is not anywhere near as lousy as it sounds. If you're riding solo, you're **inviting** people to come up and chat with you. Think of it as an interview process but this time **you're** the boss.

Keep your posture open, keep your cellphone in your purse, and act like there's nowhere else in the world that you belong more than right here and right now. You'll be surprised at how far it takes you, and who you may meet.

Learning to Pick the Good Apples from the Bad

Now that you're in charge, now that you're choosing and not being chosen, the important next step is to identify the real men from the predators. These next few tips are only part of your training. Taking the solo challenge and talking to the men that come up to you is essential if you ever want to get the differences down pat.

Sure signs of an Artist at work

Pick up artists are conversation masters. They are witty, confident, and will ask you lots of questions to get you thinking that they are interested in you as a person. They come disguised. They are often flawlessly dressed, have excellent hair, and wear cologne that will turn your brain to mush. They may also show up as a "bad boy" that has tattoos all over his body. They are capable of hitting all of your senses at once. Even the tone of their voice is meant to excite you.

They are, in effect, doing everything right—with one critical exception: they are lacking in authenticity. A guy that says something stupid by accident to you, or comes at you with a bumbling pickup line, or isn't wearing any cologne at all, is failing to impress you because he doesn't do this often enough. Pick-up artists, however, never fail. They have the right things to say to you every time, stuff that they know you ladies are prone to eat up.

If some guy is telling you all the right things, making you laugh, complimenting your eye liner, then 9 times out of 10 it's because **he's had practice at it!** Against odds like that, does it really make sense to give him what he wants in the hope that he will date you? Hell no it doesn't.

The irony is PUA's are the easiest egos (and the most fun) to deflate when you are a high value woman!

The good apples may be harder to get

The guys you want are noticeable because they are authentic. They are probably nervous when they are talking to you. They **won't** say the right things and they likely **won't** have a devilish charm and bad boy flair.

> Apply my 20-second rule.
> Give him a chance and help him out.
> He might be a great guy in 5 minutes
> when he is comfortable.

They won't be immediately obvious, either. They are playing pool, they are sitting at the bar, and they are likely watching you and trying hard as hell to keep you from noticing.

What they **will** be is real. Some aren't all that interesting, some are ugly as sin, and some don't know how to dress themselves. Your job is to find the ones that look interesting, generous, and above all authentic, and start **talking** to them. You can't know what they are like unless you're asking questions.

Of course, this brings us to a problem: how do you walk up to them. How do you engage? As stated above in the Solo Challenge Extreme Edition, once we're outside the bar scene we need to get aggressive.

Here are my five steps that any man-attracting tigress will find useful:

1) *Close the space*
First we need to make it extremely easy for the good guy. Remember we are simple creatures, so don't be afraid to dumb things down for us. A smile from across the room doesn't work. If we see that, we immediately think "she couldn't be smiling at me." Then you think "see, I smiled at him and he didn't even care...guys suck and I'm ugly."

Great, nothing has been accomplished.

Now try this: get closer. If he goes to the bar, go to the bar. If he moves to another room, then move to the room but closer. Walk past him as you hit the ladies room so you can throw in an extra look and smile. The last thing a guy wants is to be humiliated in front of his friends after walking 30 yards across a room. Make it easy and go to him.

2) *Next, Exude body language*

Smile at him – twice. Unlike women men don't pick up on positive non-verbal cues. This means you need to overdue things. Basically you need to club us over the head with a bat and yell, "I want to fucking meet you!"

3) *Strut your stuff*

At this point you have given him the green light and he may approach. If not, you approach him at the bar or, even better, you wave him over. Yes he will come!

Approach him playfully and with a smile. Ask him a question, make an observation, tell a joke or give him a challenge: "Should I get a margarita or a shot?" "Hey what do you think of that guy's shirt?" "I dare you to suck down that fruity girl's drink of yours." "Can you take my picture in front of this palm tree?"

The key is to get crazy, kill off the usual "get to know you" crap and get his squirrel brain challenged and thinking. Be spontaneous and witty like you're with your best friends. Ten minutes of having him share his favorite reality show or movie will yield a world of info relevant to building chemistry between you. Try getting that out of asking "Do you come here often?" It won't work.

Make him equate his joys **to you** and in doing so he equates joy **with you**. Psychology at work!

Make him expose things to you that he would normally reserve for his best friend. Keep him on the defensive and he will yearn for more of you. If he asks you a bland question (which he will because he's nervous) like, "how was your day?" say something like, "Awesome, my cat only shit in the litter box once and I was able to get two days out of my nail color!"

What just happened?

You just triggered **attraction**. He hasn't met a girl like you before. This immediately separates you from the heard of faceless women. Your competition is dust. The few extra pounds you have, your less-than-perfect hair, that little zit on your nose, completely melts away in his eyes at that moment. Instead of seducing his brain with sex like most women do, you seduced his **mind** and triggered an emotional connection.

4) *Next, create sexual tension*

Sexual tension is created by touching a man or making a suggestive comment like, "I go crazy for guys with tattoos, hide that will you?" These are signs that tell a man you're interested in a potential relationship and not being friends. This should happen as soon as you realize that you are interested in a man.

Tip: You should practice this flirtation often, even if you aren't interested in a man sexually, so when you meet a hot guy it will be natural. Remember, guys need to be whacked over the head to know that you are interested, and this is how you do it.

> Thousands of relationships were "almost created" last Saturday night but were not because women were sitting on their asses and not showing interest in their chosen man!

5) *Finally, close the deal*

Yes, **you** close the deal. Give him your number or ask him for his number or email and then retreat. This keeps the challenge and mystery alive.

"Here's my number, if I like you maybe we'll get together. Bye!"

That is how you get a guy to call. You kept the challenge going and kept his ego intact. In his mind he asked **you** for **your** number. You are one nasty social tigress!

You're a confident woman who has passed my Solo Challenge. You can do **anything** you set your mind to, including talking to guys. If they are with friends, enlist the aid of your girlfriends. If he's walking in the pouring rain jump under his umbrella, smile and say "how rude of me, I didn't even ask first!" If you're alone, ask him if he wants a drink. He will be stunned, he will be in awe of you, and unless he's with another girl, he **will** go to the bar with you.

And as a final piece of advice...

When you've got a guy sitting there with you, make sure you ask him questions that show his character. Ask him what his favorite movie is and what he does outside of work. Is he ambitious? Funny? Nervous? Morning person? Grumpy before coffee?

No matter what, don't be afraid to end the chat. "You're friends keep looking at you. I think they want you back at the pool table." Or "Crap, I have to take this call. Here's my number (if he's worthy) maybe I'll see you around."

At the end of the day, you need to be thinking about what's best for you. There are tons of guys at bars, and most aren't dateable. Be patient, give authentic men a chance, hone your criteria for the kind of guy that you're looking for, and strike like the social man-attracting tigress you've become.

You have become a woman of value. You no longer need validation from men. You are armed with a toolbox of traits that any man would be happy to explore- Now go find him!

Every phone has an app that you can download which provides a fake incoming call with just the press of a button.

If you get into an awkward social situation, you have an instant out with this little gem.

Challenges for Chapter 4:

Challenge:
Now that you know yourself better tell me what SPECIFIC type of guy interests you: Chivalrous, hilarious, motivated, jealous-free, holds hands, wants a family.

Challenge:
Complete my Solo Challenge with flying colors! (Extra credit for the Solo Challenge Extreme Edition!)

Challenge:
Pick out three pick-up artists at the bar, as well as three guys you think could be dateable.

Challenge:
Tell off the next pick-up artist that hits on you at a bar.

Challenge:
Go up to a guy by himself and start a conversation with him.

Challenge:
(Caution: not for the faint of heart!) Go up to a guy that is with his friends and get him to join you at the bar.

CHAPTER 5

THE SOCIAL TIGRESS IN ACTION

This is the meat and potatoes of *The Social Tigress*—You'll want to get out your highlighter for this chapter!

Ok, if you've worked hard and invested some time in yourself, you are a more confident woman. You've:

- Stepped back and realized that being single is your time to get to know yourself and what you want both in life and in a guy.

- Developed a list of potential interests and are pursuing a passion or hobby.

- Gone a full day realizing that you don't need a man to define you or your happiness.

- You've listed specific traits that you want in a man. You've smelled him, touched him and visualized the two of you together on the beach. You know who he is already.

Now we need to get aggressive like a Social Tigress and **find him, meet and attract him**. But this time we are ruling out the bar scene.

We are going to fill our bucket with men, filter out the bad ones, re-fill, filter out the so-so ones until Whammo! You've got some quality keepers in your net!

---

*QUICK NOTE: Aggressive does not mean being slutty. Slutty is defined as sleeping with every dick that comes around. Men DO NOT think women that "go on the offensive" and approach them are slutty. And don't let girls tell you otherwise. I find women feel this way towards other girls because of their highly competitive nature in a social environment. Ladies don't want other women to go after their potential marks in the room.

A) Find Him

There are 3.2 billion men out there. I'm willing to bet you walked by, drove by or even talked to what could have been your future husband today. You just didn't realize it!

I mentioned "talked to" for a reason. Never rule out a guy you already know. In my thousands of interviews with happy couples I always ask how they met. I am amazed that the answer usually sounds like: "I didn't really like him at first." This means the men they fell for took a little bit of time to grow on them.

Many women tell me that they know in the first five seconds if there is chemistry with a man. I challenge you, as part of your training, to question this premise. I see so many relationships that are DOA even though sparks were flying the first week or two. Love, I feel, takes time and grows day by day with a special person. This type of relationship tends to be the kind that lasts. So don't rule out someone that might already be in your life or doesn't peak your interest immediately.

Now, back to finding men! As I mentioned before, that number is 3.2 billion. You literally have a Super Target Store of single men out there, so let's find the bastards!

Let's have a little fun here; let's say you just bought a pair of new red shoes. All of a sudden you start noticing all the girls that are wearing red shoes. Red shoes are all over the place. Now did women just start buying more red shoes or did you just start noticing them?

The answer? It really doesn't matter. The fact is you see more red shoes in your life.

Tomorrow morning I want you to start noticing all the single men (red shoes) that you encounter throughout your day.

Finding Men is as simple as 1, 2...and that's it!
- Know the style of man you want to meet
- Go to the venue where this type of man will likely be

Step #1 –
Know the style of man you want to meet

You already know his style and what you desire. You have listed his traits. You know what you have to have and what you can compromise on. Men come in a basket of characteristics like a box of chocolates. You will never find the perfect mix, nor will he with you, but look at the entire basket at what he has to offer.

A confident girl, aka **you**, can get her **significant** other to experiment and bring out different traits that they never knew existed. Bad boys can become very cultured and geeks can get crazy on a motorcycle **if** their trusted partner believes in them. The same holds true for a guy towards you.

My point being, don't rule out a man because you feel he is missing some of the traits you desire by judging him on the outside. In a strong trusting relationship fantasies get explored and traits that sit idle inside can be brought to the forefront.

"But men don't change Gregg!"

Men don't change when they have an **insignificant** partner. You are not insignificant. As I teach in *Who Holds the Cards Now?*, if you become his prize you can get any man to change in any way you want him to for a lifetime! And I'm not talking about putting down the toilet seat here.

Sure, look for the characteristics you need but realize they will never **all** be there.

Step #2 –
Go to the venue where
this type of man will likely be

Let's say you are interested in a very well-travelled and cultured man. Are you going to hit the nightclub? You could but that would be a waste of time. And if by some miracle you met your well-travelled, cultured man at a club, what is he going to think of you? You want to meet this type of guy at an International Living Magazine seminar (great magazine by the way), wine tasting event, the Museum of Fine Art, a Broadway show or a course on learning how to speak French.

I hate to be blatantly obvious here but women overlook this fact every day. The first question I ask a lonely attractive woman is what does her social life consist of and all I get is," nightclubs, bars and Starbucks." The next question I ask her is what type of man she is interested in and I get," tall, dark and handsome." I don't even bother with the next question, "What type of girl are you?" My answer will be, "Duh, I don't know, I wanna be loved."

Go to where the source is! You need water, go to a river. You like sand, hit the beach - don't climb a tree.

You want affluent? Hit charity events, fine restaurant bars, the opera or classic Ferrari club event.

You want a risk taker? Take a white water rafting trip, ride a zip line, skydive or bungee jump.

You love bikers? Get your license, buy a chopper, hit up biker venues.

Looking for someone spiritual? Go to church, take a hot yoga course, meditation class or a bible reading course.

Music? Hit small concert venues, go online and sign up for turntable, learn to play an instrument.

You crave the jock? Hit the gym, do Crossfit, run a marathon, enter a bike race, do P90X online.

By going directly to the source you gain several advantages:

- You share a common interest and can engage in a mutually pleasing conversation immediately.

- Barriers are relaxed because neither of you are on the "you're trying to pick me up" defensive.

- Unlike a bar, there are very few distractions so you can get to know each other in peace.

- You are likely to see this person again so it's not necessary to set up a potential nerve-wracking date. For instance, a yoga class will allow you to see the same interesting guy automatically in one week.

Nothing worthwhile comes without a fight. This means you need to get outside your comfort zone and dig into these venues. Remember, you are single because you are staying inside your safe zone. What you already have in life is **in** your safe zone. You want what you don't have – now get out there!

B) Meet and Attract Him

"I wish for the love of God that women would walk up to me!" That's not just me speaking—that's every heterosexual guy on earth crying out. I teach chapter after chapter to men about the approach, but with you it's **easy**... Just do anything and we will jump up and down with happiness and pee our pants in shock. We have enormously fragile egos that need to be protected at all costs and this applies especially when we are with our friends, so if you come to us...Yeah!

Women don't approach men. It is rare, therefore it is highly effective and you will have no competition in the room. Use this to your advantage. You make the effort and we will take over. In my best selling book, *The Building of a Confident Man*, I teach men that they get hit on all the time and it's true. You ladies constantly hit on us but in such subtle ways we usually don't notice. You give us glances, smiles, hair tosses and may even take a detour to the ladies room but it's **not** enough. Men are used to rejection from women so we need stronger and more obvious cues from you.

In fact, studies show that high-signaling average looking women will get approached more often than low-signaling highly attractive women. Use this fact. Don't sit on your ass and wait. Spot those available men and let loose the Social Tigress within!

Different men will respond to different signals, so your mission is to pick a single or combination of body language cues from my list below that work for you (and him.)

- Look over at him and quickly look away multiple times. Some men will lock on to this cue.

- Make eye contact with him. Make eye contact again but add a smile. It's the second eye contact that is most important as this gives validation that you are specifically interested in him. This should work in most cases.

- Same as above but now turn towards him keeping your shoulders square. We just added another layer of intent.

- Walk by him and physically touch him on the arm or shoulder as if you accidentally bumped into him. All men will respond to this, most positively.

- Nuclear option: wave his ass over! I mean it. This is especially successful when he is with his friends. You are **inflating** his ego in front of everyone...kudos my Social Tigress!

Make it extra easy for men to approach you

Do's and Don'ts:

- *Do go out alone or keep it to three max.*
  Only pros will approach a pack of wolves.

- *Don't wear outfits that are too revealing.*
  There are three reasons for this:

  a) If you show too many body parts guys will get intimidated and will not approach (proven by women in bikinis at the beach—men rarely have the balls to approach a half-naked woman.)

  b) If you exude sex, a man's brain will be hijacked and he will only want sex from you.

  c) Save that sexy outfit and impress him when you are out on the date.

- *Do create space next to you.*
  This is one that most ladies overlook. A man needs an opening to talk to you and he would prefer something private—especially with his opening line in case he gets shot down. Leave an empty seat next to you or if you're standing, leave space. We will not approach if you are in a crowded isle.

- *Don't be on the move.*
  How many men have approached you while you are on the move? Likely, it's not many. When you see an opportunity (which you are looking for now - red shoes) stop and maybe sit on a park bench or jump in a line. If you're at the grocery store stop and get something right next to him.

  Never underestimate the power of a waiting line.

- *Don't go out with other men if you're on the hunt.*
  I don't care if it's your brother or your dad. A man will

assume the guy's your boyfriend or husband. They will immediately write you off and look for other women. Many guys don't like other guys entering their space and men know and respect this except the PUA's.

- *Do wear something flamboyant or something that stands out.*

  This little gem gives guys a reason to approach. I teach men to look for what I call SAL's, or Situational Approach Lines. For you, this could be a scarf, a hat, a puppy, purple highlights in your hair, anything that will help you stand out from other women. Need proof? Go out this weekend with a pair or crutches and watch what happens. I will guarantee that so many men will say something you'll be using them for kindling.

Preparation and Intent

Wow, you are making great progress! Now let's talk about preparation. You need a plan for when you meet this guy because you're sure as hell on your way to doing so. Everything I teach goes up in a cloud of smoke if your knees buckle and you start to drool when that attractive man says something.

Let's talk about intent. If your intent is to go out with this gorgeous guy and make him your boyfriend, you put a lot of pressure on yourself and thus you might blow it. So what do you do? Change your intent, of course. If you walk up to that same guy and ask him where the best place to go after a wine tasting is then you change your intent and the pressure is off. Use this trick and you will be better prepared.

Here's another way to prepare: date three guys at one time. This places you in a position of abundance and not scarcity. Most women live in scarcity. They have few choices of men so they compromise. If you date several men (I say date, you don't have to sleep with them!) good things happen:

- You get a lot of dating practice and can think clearly what you want in a man. The dynamics of relationships become crystal clear.

- Rejection hurts much less because you have two waiting in the wings.

- You become less needy and aloof by default. You can't be with all three (well you can but that's another subject entirely) so you inevitably say no to men.

- This in turn creates a challenge for your Three Wiseman and they start to want you more...wow, talk about the domino effect!

Time to Talk

Unlike men, it's pretty hard for women to screw up. In fact I don't need to give you any pick-up lines. Say something, anything, to a man, and the guy takes over unless he is totally shy. Usually the problem is getting him to shut up. At a bar, I tell women to keep it simple: ask him advice, ask him for help, challenge, tease, or comment on his watch.

But Gregg, tonight we are not at the bar!

You are correct. Tonight you are at an upgraded venue of **your** choosing and you are about to talk to a high value man (or at least your chances are greatly increased.) Your start-up conversation should be easy because you have the same interest at this venue such as wine tasting or supporting a common charity. Your goal is to make both of you comfortable, then steer the conversation to things that you need him to share to see if he is worthy of dating. Forget the job, forget the weather, and stick to the important stuff!

With this higher value man I want you to do a few things differently. You are sharing a common interest so have an opinion, ask him his and then challenge it. Do this while being playful and with a smile. Smart men **need** this challenge, they rarely find it and they aren't used to it. When they are challenged their sexual endorphins kick in and they want more from you.

This leads to an emotional connection and this, my dear, is the road to **attraction** and a lasting relationship.

Remember to balance the conversation. Don't get competitive. Don't be overly passive and agree with everything (like most women do.)

The intangible attraction, your secret ingredient

These following paragraphs are going to get deep. They are one of the most important items in this book as I try to define how you can trigger a man's inner attraction. I know the answer. God do I know the answer, but I don't know if I can convey it to you. This can only be described by a man witnessing the grace of a woman.

Throughout my day I study and talk to people. I study their moves and their interactions as I try to learn the dynamics of interpersonal relationships. It's my job.

Every now and then I see a woman that is doing something cute. She may slip a little in her heels and react in such a way. She might be interacting with her girlfriend and make a dancing gesture that's funny. She may be licking an ice cream and lose a scoop on the ground. She may pat a dog and speak in her puppy talk voice. But it is unique and cute to her.

I describe this force as an intangible, unpredictable quality that is unique to all women. It is almost always something simple—an everyday occurrence to everyone and yet, somehow, someway, **you** make it cute. It's your innocence that is showing. In such a tough, complicated world, your "display or small screw up" makes us melt and realize what matters in life and why we are here. It is why we yearn to come home to you at night.

You have what I am trying to describe. Now bring it out as soon as you can to a man. Let him see you and all of your inner goodness as fast as you can. This means you need to be comfortable and at peace with yourself. Talk to this new man like you are old friends and show him who you are. Be silly, feisty, laugh at him and yourself. Stay positive and above all stay unpredictable and keep him guessing. Men love nothing more than not knowing what this girl in front of him is going to do!

If you do this, this intangible trait that I am describing will pour out of you and he will see. And he will think, "This is my future, standing right in front of me."

If you do what I explain above, men will see what I am talking about and you will have done what I set out for you to do by default!

The "I'm in charge temporarily" attraction

I love this one and women get great results. I go out with girls and I set up this challenge in a bar (I like bars for this exercise because they are so informal) and the results are amazing.

A high value man likes to take control. In fact, rarely does a woman come along to reverse this trend. While you are interacting with your new man at your common venue, I want you to grab his hand and say, "come on Mr. Bob (use whatever his first name is preceded by Mr., makes it fun) let's go get a drink, or let's go look at the next exhibit, or let's try eating this chocolate covered bug."

This attracts a high value man on many levels:

1) You surprised him. Rarely, does he get surprised and this attracts him. As stated above this fits into the "keep him guessing" and "unpredictability" categories that men crave but rarely witness.

2) You exude confidence with one single move. This tells him that you know what you want and you go for it.

3) He thinks, "hmm, what else is she going to do?" He will stick around to find out.

After you deploy this tactic, it's important to go passive. Let him get back to what he does best (be in control) and then hit him again. Basically you're playing with him. You're saying, "you don't intimidate me like you do other women." This works like the bomb!

Balance is everything so go in and out of being passive. If you continue to lead him around the room you will come across as just plain bossy.

Conclusion to Find, Meet and Attract

At this point you should never be asking me the age old question, "Why can't I find a guy?" No longer are you heading out with horse blinders on looking for a man.

What I have given you is more tools in your toolbox; your confidence should be on the rise because you have defined yourself, explored a passion and now know the traits in a man you desire. No longer are bars and clubs your mainstay. You are patronizing specific venues where **your** particular type of man is likely to be found. Because of this, talking to him on a mutual subject is very easy. You have learned body language cues to attract him and engage.

You realize you have a great advantage over other women because you can now go on the offensive. You go out alone on occasion, dress down and wear something that draws attention so men have an excuse to approach. And you know that you need to create space next to you and stay in one place. You leave the guy friends at home.

I have also given you the secret ingredient and a few goodies that will make him crave more of you.

You are becoming a complete and utterly invincible **SOCIAL TIGRESS** and I bow to you!

Only One Challenge:
Read over this chapter one more time. Go out and string together as many tips as you can above. Know that the first time out you will screw up some things but that's OKAY. These little screw ups are your secret ingredient that he will love!

CHAPTER 6

FORGET THE GUESSWORK: MEETING MEN ON YOUR TERMS

Getting Past the Bar Stools and Bar Fools

You're upgraded. You're You 2.0. And with your new confidence and your newfound interest in **finding** your interests, it's time to promote **more** smart techniques that will get you meeting and interacting with more men on a constant basis.

With that said I want you to answer a serious question: how many men do you engage in one week? Let's qualify this. How many men do you talk to in a REAL conversation? I'm not talking about the guy who rings up your groceries or delivers your UPS packages (unless he's real hot). I'm talking about a guy that you could potentially see yourself with.

Have your answer? Great. Now, I'm not a betting man...but if I were, I would bet your answer was zero, zilch, nada, possibly one, but that one guy was probably at a bar, and he was a loser or a pick-up artist. It's alright, that's completely common.

So given these facts, and being completely honest with yourself, how in HELL are you going to find the man of your dreams?

The cold hard truth is...YOU WON'T! You simply can't! If you're going to meet men, you need to put yourself out there. And it can't be purely at bars. You must meet them in lots of places. To help you with this, I wrote up a chapter that gives you tips on **where** and **how** to meet men. Inevitably, as you increase in value and develop your interests, you'll realize that you don't want to meet just **any** man, anywhere—you want to meet a man that is as valuable as you are that shares the same interests as you do.

Ready to get to work? Excellent! Let's get right into it, starting with my five surefire ways to meet men.

Gregg's 5 Surefire Ways to Meet Men

Below is a list of five methods that will immediately get you meeting and talking to men in natural settings that are far removed from the bar. Leave your comfort zone, get out there, and start making things happen—because if you decide just to wait for the man of your dreams to come to you, you may be waiting a long, long time.

Volunteer at your local singles events club

This is a great one and you may be able to stop the quest for your knight right here. All across the States are specialized groups with the sole purpose of helping you meet other singles in the area. These are NOT dating sites. They're cool activities and social venues strung together just for singles. Hell, you may even be able to get paid if you really want to throw time into it.

Think about it: every guy you come across at these events you **know** is single. I have done many of these events and met a lot of people. And no, this is **not** the land of misfit toys. These are **smart**, good looking men that don't want to peruse the bars and clubs where the sharks hang out. They aren't looking for sluts. They are looking for women with value and character.

Many of these venues have two or three events per week. Go for it and live in the world of abundance instead of scarcity. Here you have **choice** and plenty of it!

P.S: Volunteering is way better than going as just another single guy or gal. This way you can flirt with guys, but you don't need to feel out of place because you're actually working the event.

In my area, Boston MA, and all over the country is a singles event club called Events and Adventures. This is one of the larger singles groups in the States, and it comes highly recommended! Even if it doesn't operate in your area, don't give up hope. There are plenty of other quality choices when it comes to singles clubs.

Sports anyone?

You don't need me to say it, but I'll say it anyway: **go to SPORTS bars!** The ratio is massively in your favor.

"But Gregg, I **hate** sports! Why are you making me do this?" Because it's good for you! And in any case, you don't really hate sports; you hate how your last asshole boyfriend spent his time watching them instead of being attentive to you. But now you've read my Amazon best seller, *Who Holds the Cards Now?*, so you have solved this problem.

We guys **love** to teach women stuff; it's practically in our DNA. It makes us feel fulfilled and worthy. If you go to a Sports Bar and ask a few questions you will MEET men and, hell, may find that you actually like whatever game is playing! Now sure you'll get the occasional dick that won't say "boo" to you because he is so engrossed—but you don't want this loser anyway.

I'll even challenge you further: learn the game! My last girl-friend, Kim, didn't have a clue how it was played. So I pa-tiently took her under my wing, and when it was just the two of us, I'd take out a laser pointer, make it fun, and re-joice when I saw her eyes light up.

And really, at the end of the day, if you can't beat them, join them. You'll be amazed at how far that saying can take you. Start thinking outside the box, and hit up Nascar races, hockey games, and MMA matches: no matter where you go, men are bound to be drawn to you.

Be a stalker

No, I don't mean a real stalker. But redirect your path towards that handsome man that you often come across. You see a cute guy grabbing an ice cream? Grab an ice cream. He's headed up the elevator? Jump in. He's looking interested in the news on TV? Get interested at the same time. Who cares if it changes your original plan or makes no sense or it takes 5 minutes extra of your time. Big deal! This 5 minute re-route could be the guy you marry.

Imagine the possibilities! Stalking just one guy a day would lead to seven new men a week that you can strike up a conversation with outside the nasty bar scene. Almost instantly you've become a chooser, which is exactly how I want you to operate going forward.

Cut in line

I have to throw this one in. It's definitely aggressive, but by now you know you're a social tigress ready to **pounce** at any chance to meet a good man. Choosers take risks and don't sit back on their stilettos. However, if are super shy then you'll probably want to sit this one out. You won't get an ear full from me, I promise!

We wait in lines our entire life so let's take advantage of this. Look for the cute guy or guys in the line ahead of you. Walk up and ask him if you can go in with him. Tell him you will pay for yourself. Be cute. Say, "Hey, you look like you need a date tonight!" I guarantee any decent single man will be excited to let you join him. And if he doesn't, who gives a crap!

Now, guys can't do this but women can. Chivalry lives and boring ass waiting lines are the way to bring this characteristic out. Trust me, I am that decent single guy and if you ask me, I'll say yes every time. Oh, and if its pouring rain and you happen to jump under my umbrella with me? Awesome!

Enjoy the hell out of being single

You're single and you want to meet a man. I understand. But many women feel like they are losers or terrible people because their friends are all married or in relationships. **Stop** this thought process right now. Being single is an awesome part of being alive and can be **fun**. Make it this way.

I've read a thousand online dating profiles, and the ones that state how tired they are of being single make me want to puke! They make it sound like being single is a disease. It's not! Follow my advice and the journey to a relationship will be exciting.

In concluding up my 5 tips...

I do these things in my everyday life to meet women and it's a howl! There is nothing more romantic than talking about how you met throwing a ball at a clown at some lame town fair compared to, say, online. Or admitting, later, that you went 45 stories up the stupid elevator when your office floor is the second! And even when you fail because the guy was a total stiff it's a mini-adventure that makes you better person.

Now sit down and brainstorm ahead of time where you can multiply my advice above. These may sound like silly trivial suggestions but they **can't** be overlooked. I mean, really, why not go into Starbucks instead of your usual drive through where there is **no** way to meet a man? Don't compartmentalize your social life into Friday and Saturday nights. Start Monday morning, and by the weekend you'll be thanking me.

Quick Note on Online Dating

While online dating is not in the scope of this book, it can be a smart (and safe) way of meeting men. It's also immediately attractive to you shy gals out there who are looking at the tips in this book and breaking out in the sweats. Yes, my book has some bold tips in it, but the big takeaway from all of this is that just by **doing** them you vastly improve your confidence. The same can't be said of safely checking out pictures and bios on your computer in your pajamas.

Online dating has improved by leaps and bounds over the last few years. Whereas you once had to wade through thousands of random faces, you can now join dating sites that are very specific, where you can find men with interests and passions similar to your own. Join more than one site and don't sweat it if that hot guy that's writing you suddenly stops. One quick look will show you the thousands of other guys that are free for taking.

Dating sites don't make you immune to pick-up artist charm. I have known guys to juggle dozens of women both online and offline. An internet platform gives them the ability to send out mass messages. It makes things way too easy for them, so make sure you keep your guard up even if he seems like the nicest person in the world.

That's a Wrap for Chapter Six

How are you feeling? Confident? Excited? Are you anticipating your first stalking experience? Do I dare say that you are? If so, then congratulations! You're on the road to becoming the woman of value you've always wanted to be.

And the truth is that we're almost done! There's just one final chapter that stands between you and total dating dominance. In Chapter Seven, I give you a brief look into the art of dating, and how to knock those first few dates out of the park.

Ready to step your dating game up one more notch? Good then! Let's get to it!

Challenges for Chapter 6:

Challenge:
Sign up for a volunteer position at a local singles group.

Challenge:
Go to a sport's bar by yourself and watch the next big football game. Make sure to get there early enough to get a good seat. (Extra credit for asking the guys around you questions!)

Challenge:
Sign up for two NON GENERAL dating sites and write at least one profile of yourself and what you're looking for in a guy.

Challenge:
"Stalk" at least three guys this week, with extra credit if you can ask them a related question to what's going on (Uh...is that catsup or ketchup over there?)

CHAPTER 7

THE FIRST DATES MADE SIMPLE

You've Done It! You're Practically There!

Look at how far you've come! You've identified and possibly even pursued a number of potential interests. Along the way you've met some cool people, developed a newfound confidence, and improved the art of spotting out the loser guys from the winners. Seriously, this is tangible stuff that is going to take your love life farther than you ever realized!

But...this *is* a dating book, right?

I've gone on so long about how you need to develop your single skills that you're probably asking yourself this question right about now. Yes, the book is about dating—but we went at it from an entirely different perspective, first starting with confidence building, and then developing the skills you need to find **good** men. I am absolutely certain that these skills come first, and once you've developed them, dating becomes way easier, and so does maintaining a relationship for that matter.

But I understand that you ladies could use a few pointers when you're out on those initial first dates. And that is what this chapter is all about.

Before I begin imparting my dating wisdom upon all of you gorgeous gals however, I want to go over three simple little facts about dating that will make your life **a million times easier** if you keep them in mind.

First:
Never, ever forget that dating is just that: dating

Dating is not marriage. Dating is not marriage. Dating is not marriage. Dating, ladies, is neither binding nor permanent. It is a time to **experiment** with different people. Learn about traits that you like and traits you don't like. Becoming too connected at this stage, especially while young, is almost always a bad idea.

Because dating is not a binding agreement, you can date other people. You can draw the line at intimacy or not. I'm not in the business of giving you moral advice. What I can tell you is that going on just a standard date or two with someone while you're dating someone else is more than just okay. It's good for you. If it makes another guy jealous, all the better.

Second:
Dating isn't an excuse to drop your interests

If you find a guy in the next couple of weeks and drop everything to be with him, chances are you will continue to entrap yourself in the same cycle again and again. Oh, you'll find a long-term relationship eventually, but without those interests on the side you'll never hold the cards in the relationship. This is why I'm adamant about you following through with being single, at least for a while!

If, however, you're committed to the dating scene, then at least do yourself a favor and **keep looking for your interests!** I cannot stress how important this is in your own life and the life you have with your future boyfriend or potential husband. If you simply give up searching, you will forever be beholden to the same unhealthy hubby addiction that you've always had. You've set an example to this man entering the relationship that you have other hobbies than him and these interests will continue with or without him.

Third:
End the "I hate playing games" mantra that's on replay in your head

I can't count the amount of times I've heard something along the lines of: "I just don't get why I need to ignore how I feel. Why can't I just express myself and stop playing all the games? If I think I love someone after the first date why can't I just come out and say it!"

I think most of us know the reason. We run the risk of ruining the relationship if we show our hand too quickly. We need time to gauge the interest of the other person, and that means putting up smokescreens here and there to see what they'll do and how they'll act. But instead of getting angry and saying how much you hate the games, you need to do the complete opposite and *embrace* them when it's necessary. My best seller *Who Holds the Cards Now?* covers these "games" in great detail. Games need to be played only on occasion when your man goes what I call "rogue."

You simply need to realize that being indirect with someone has its benefits, and that the benefits outweigh the misunderstandings that ensue from being direct! For example, let's say you see a hot guy and "accidentally" drop your pen next to him. He immediately goes to pick it up, you say something silly like, "oh, how clumsy of me." In doing so, he thinks it's his idea that you met. He begins a conversation that leads to a date.

Why is it important that he think that? Because to the mind of a man, if it's easy to get, it isn't very valuable. If you convince us that we had to fight tooth and nail to get to you, then there's a good chance we will never leave you. Simply put, at times you **must** play games. Not just because we like them, but because our brains are programmed that way. There's no point in asking why this is. But if you don't embrace it, you're going to have a tough time dating.

Your Field Guide to the First Few Dates

The first few two or three dates are important steps on your way to developing a relationship. In many cases you'll know by date one or two whether you want to keep seeing the person. In fact, you'll probably know within the first hour of sitting down with them if you want to see them again. Your job, of course, is to keep the playing field open. You've got all the time in the world, and a lot more guys to date before you settle on just one!

The way I set this segment up was in question/answer format. Basically it's a list of the most commonly asked questions to the first few dates, followed by my (expert!) advice. You'll find plenty of gold here, so keep reading, and soon enough you'll be unleashing the social tigress that's bottled up within you!

Gregg, do I put out on the first (or second, or third) date?

No. And double no if you really like him. The truth is if you have sex with him on the first date, he'll probably take you up on your offer. But that does **not** mean that he will keep seeing you. In fact, he's all the more likely to **not** see you again.

Why you ask? Because you gave him what he wanted way too fast. Sex, whether you like it or not, is the ace up your sleeve. Use it wisely, and you can win the game. Use it at the wrong time, and it will quickly work against you.

Remember: guys have to **work** for something in order to make it worthwhile for them. **Do not try to fight this!** This is how our physiology works; this is how we feel regardless of how you **think** we should feel. There's no point in trying to make it work any other way, because it will never happen! The takeaway from this is that if you give in too fast, you will be used and left in the dust. Don't do this to yourself. Save it for later if you like the guy.

A guy wants to feel that **he** is special in the eyes of his woman. If you sleep with him the first night he feels that you do this with every guy and he's not special. If you wait a couple of weeks and **then** sleep with him, he'll feel like he worked for you. Make him work for you.

So when should you give it to him?

When he has proven his worth and both of you have made an emotional connection and you feel comfortable.

Furthermore, I want three more things out of you and him before you sleep together; I want you to meet his friends. I want him to meet your friends. And third, I want you to see what he is like when he is drunk and you're not! These three items are covered in depth in my relationship book *Who Holds the Cards Now?*. If you want to understand the reasons behind these three beauties, and you should, grab my other book for the price of a cup of coffee (the diner kind, not the Starbucks kind).

If a guy really likes you, he will stick around for quite a while (within reason!) without getting any. And seriously...if he stops calling because you're not putting out, how big of a loss is it, really?

Gregg, what the hell do I talk about with him?

If there's an elephant in the room during the first date or two, it's the fear of an awkward silence. Mere seconds without someone talking is physical anguish on par with torture techniques used by the Spanish Inquisition.

I can't be there at your next big date whispering in your ear what you should be telling him. What I CAN do is tell you to stop worrying about just one date so much! Sometimes you'll meet guys that are your polar opposites. Almost always, if you search enough, you'll find something in common to talk about. Really though, your initial chitchat is all about how you *feel* when you're talking to him. Is he being friendly? Is he *trying* to keep you engaged? Is he courteous without being a prude?

Since it's the first date, try to introduce topics that mean something to you. Do you want a man with a solid family behind him? Ask him about his family upbringing and how often he sees his parents. Do you want an educated man? Ask him about what he did in college (or if he went at all). Do you want someone adventurous? Ask him if he plays sports, goes on hikes, or has lived abroad. Find the things that are most important to you and start seeing whether you're a good match or not.

Test him. Men love nothing more than to talk about themselves. Get him talking about himself and see if he can shut up and get back to **your** interests. If he can he could be a keeper as he is showing signs of unselfishness which is a rare trait in men these days. This is a great test!

If he's looking at other women, or is full of himself, get the hell out. He won't argue with you if you say you have a mean case of the period cramps. Otherwise stay polite and give him a chance if he's trying to find common ground with you. If you get desperate you can tell him you have 50 cats and want 25 more and that should make him wrap up the evening. I mean do you really want to date a guy that can't even hold a conversation for ten minutes? Or checks out other women? Or is full of his own shit?

Remember, your time is valuable now and you don't have time to waste it with guys that are not a match. Give him a chance, root him on but know when a guy is wasting your night and exit.

What turns you off during a date Gregg?

Probably the same things that would turn you off if it happened during a first date: the person arrives super late; they're dressed just plain wrong or insist on being rude to the waiter; they're constantly bombarding you with "I don't know. What do *you* want to do" comments over the phone. They have no substance, they have no value and they bring no challenge. This stuff is pretty much self-explanatory and I doubt any of you are silly enough to do any of it.

But if you're guilty of arriving completely stoned to your date after making him wait 30 minutes, and then singing Brittany Spears at the top of your lungs while he drives you to a café for dessert, you probably need more help than I can give you (yes, I know the guy that this really happened to).

Should he pay, or should we split the bill?

Chivalry still lives in the hearts of men, and many of us feel it our rightful duty to foot the tab for the first few dates. And as a free spirited, completely liberated woman, you may very well take offense to his urgent need to do so. My personal suggestion is that when the bill comes, you simply **ask** if he would like to split it. If he says no, you **gracefully** acquiesce to his decision.

If you feel really uncomfortable, tell him that you'll only go on another date with him if you get to pay (that is, of course, if you want to see him again. Otherwise, enjoy the free meal!) If, however, he says YES to the split, don't get all disgruntled over it! Plenty of guys out there don't want to cause an argument. If you ask to split it, don't be offended if he actually does it.

My personal feeling is if he asks you out than he pays. If you ask him out he still should pay! But that's me, I hate cheap guys and you have soo many choices now - why date a cheap loser?

Taking Care of a Few Loose Ends

And so concludes the wisdom of Chapter 7. By this point you should be ready to take on the dating scene with an entirely different perspective. Not only do you have what it takes to **find** men that are actually worth something, but you are confident enough and valuable enough to impress the hell out of them.

You also know how to treat those first few dates. You know all about what cards you need to keep, and which you can throw on the table. You know that asking the right questions on those first few dates are essential to learning his character and that you never have to put up with someone that isn't showing as much interest in you as he should be.

Finally, you deserve a **standing ovation** for making it as far as you have. You've come a long way since Chapter 1. As you hit the challenges for Chapter 7, make sure you use every bit of what you've learned to complete them successfully!

Challenges for Chapter 7:

Challenge:
On your next big date, **you** steer the conversation in the direction that you want. That means you need to be the one asking questions and follow-ups. Get specific! Hit on a topic and delve into it. Test him, play with him. Act silly and tease him. These are the traits that men **love**.

Challenge:
Either with an online method or in your daily life, go out on a date with three **completely** different guys in a two week period. I want to see you take out a bad boy, a dweeb and a guy way younger or older so you can get a baseline comparison reading of what turns you on...I guarantee you will be surprised and enlightened! (Extra credit if you do it at the same restaurant each time. Haha!)

Challenge:
Relish the games! Tell a guy you're dating that you're seeing a few other guys at the same time, and you're just testing out the waters. Then, tell him you'll call him the next day and don't. What will happen? Calls, calls and more calls because you are making these men work for you! Boo yah!

Challenge:
Refuse a date due to either a class or something else related specifically to your new interest. ("I can't go out Saturday night. I have a wine tasting to go to. How about Sunday?")

A BIT ABOUT

YOUR DRILL SERGEANT

Hi I'm Gregg.

I'm one of Boston's top dating coaches. I'm a little crazy (maybe a lot), I break rules, I get bored easy and I help girls and guys get a clue.

I won't bore you with my professional bio. Instead I think you would prefer to hear my story of how I became a dating coach and what makes me qualified to coach you.

The irony is I came from a highly dysfunctional family. I saw my parents crumble before my eyes at an early age. Flying dishes seemed normal in my household. I came out a bit angry and proved it with 12 years of failed relationships.

But I started seeing positive things in my life too. I saw that couple, that elusive elderly couple holding hands in the park at the ripe old age of eighty. And it gave me hope! I am a problem solver and I can solve anything (I thought)...except relationships damn it!

After a long stretch of being single, in 2009 I had an epiphany. I WANTED ANSWERS TO LOVE. I decided to study my failures and interview as many single people and couples as I could. I needed to find the secret to FINDING the right person and making it last. And do you know where I started? You guessed it, those elusive elderly happy couples!

Since then, I've talked with thousands of couples; happy couples, unhappy couples, single people of all types and everything in between.

I went to work and my friends noticed. They actually pushed me to start a dating advice website so I did. I started coaching guys. Now I own the top dating site for men; KeysToSeductions.com. My site has exploded.

Why? Because I give REAL dating advice that average men (and women) can use! Let's face it, if you have GQ looks or the body and face of a model then you don't need my help.

I listen to women. They blog on my site and help us guys attract and date quality girls. Women love us too because they get a better selection of men that "GET IT!"

Today, after thousands of interviews, I have done it...I have broken the code and I am in a great relationship myself because of it. Now I want to share my findings with YOU!

Lately, I have moved into writing and coaching women. The truth is that it was a natural next step. Being completely sincere here: I love and respect women, I honestly do. I have no interest in manipulating them, nor would I ever need to. Over the years I have listened to what women have to say. I know them inside and out. My skills were honed at an early age. I just didn't know it. I was the little runt in my family - I have three older sisters and I am the only boy.

I've been doing the dating coach thing for so long now that it's safe to say I understand what gets under your skin, and what the biggest problems are with your dating lives.

I now have eleven Amazon Best Sellers, two of which are #1 Best Sellers. I am not a writer but I sure as HECK can show you how to FIND a great guy and stay happy with him for a long time!

Today I travel and teach in all the sexy playgrounds; LA, South Beach and Las Vegas. Call me Hitch or call me Gregg but just call me and watch how we can transform YOUR dating life or HELP your current relationship. I don't just write best sellers - I like to talk directly to my readers and I do as often as I can. My readers are my friends. I am humble and I want to help you.

So join me in my quest to SOLVE your dating problems and place you on a NEW and exciting path to an extraordinary relationship!

Gregg Michaelsen
Confidence Builder

MORE BOOKS
BY GREGG MICHAELSEN

For Women

Who Holds the Cards Now?
5 Lethal Steps to Win His Heart and Get Him to Commit

Power Texting Men!
The Best Texting Attraction Book to Get the Guy

Love is in the Mouse!
Online Dating for Women: Crush Your Rivals
and Start Dating Extraordinary Men

Committed to Love, Separated by Distance:
How to Thrive in Your Long Distance Relationship

Be Quiet and Date Me!
Dating for Introverts in a World That Never Stops Talking

How to Get Your Ex Back Fast!
Toy with the Male Psyche and Get Him Back
with Skills only a Dating Coach Knows

For Men

From Zero to Hero: A Modern Guys Guide to
Understanding a Womans Heart (with Kat Kingston)

Hook, Line & Date Her: The Average Guy's Book to
Attract, Meet and Date Quality Women

The Building of a Confident Man: How to Create Self
Esteem and Become More Attractive to Women

Find them on Amazon today!